GW01551133

MACMILLAN
HEINEMANN
English Language Teaching

Smile please! 4

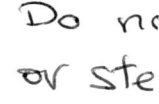

Workbook

Gabby Pritchard
Additional material by Jeanne Perrett-Tamami

Unit 1   I'm from Britain.

1. Look, read and answer.

1. I'm from Britain. I'm British. Who am I? __Anna__

2. I'm from Canada. Who am I? _____

3. I'm Japanese. Who am I? _____

2. Sort and write.

1. name/What's/?/your

_____

2. Ken/name's/My/.

_____

3. from/?/you/are/Where/Anna/,

_____

4. from/I'm/./Britain

_____

5. ./British/I'm

_____

3. Find and write.

| Japan | British | ~~Greece~~ | Canada | Canadian | Britain | Japanese | ~~Greek~~ |

Greek _____ _____ _____

Greece _____ _____ _____

4. Draw and write about yourself.

My name's _____

_____

I'm from _____

_____

I'm _____

_____

5. Look, read and complete.

Name: <u>Akiko</u>

Age: <u>14</u>

Nationality: <u>Japanese</u>

Lives in: _____

Speaks: _____ and English

Name: <u>Dimos</u>

Age: <u>10</u>

Nationality: <u>Greek</u>

Lives in: _____

Speaks: _____ and English

Name: <u>Pablo</u>

Age: _____

Nationality: <u>Spanish</u>

Lives in: <u>Madrid</u>

Speaks: _____ and English

Name: _____

Age: <u>20</u>

Nationality: _____

Lives in: <u>Toronto</u>

Speaks: <u>French and</u> _____

6. Correct these sentences.

1. Dimos is British.
   <u>No. Dimos is Greek.</u>

2. Jane is from Spain.

   _____

3. Pablo speaks French.

   _____

4. Akiko lives in Toronto.

   _____

5. Dimos lives in Madrid.

   _____

7. Read and complete.

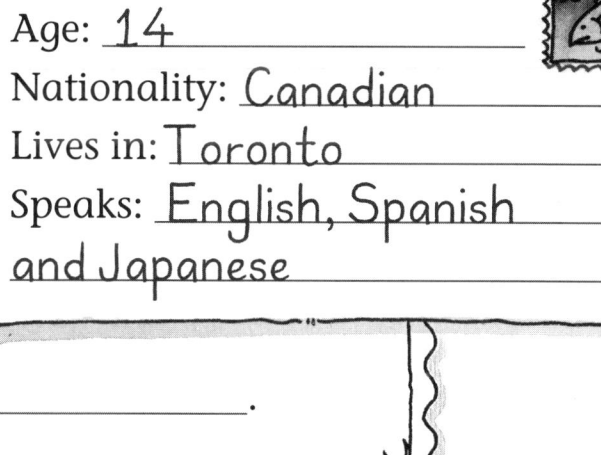

Name: <u>Jack</u>
Age: <u>14</u>
Nationality: <u>Canadian</u>
Lives in: <u>Toronto</u>
Speaks: <u>English, Spanish and Japanese</u>

Dear Maria,

My name's _____.

I'm _____ years old and I live

in _____. I'm _____.

I speak _____, _____

and _____.

Please write soon. <u>Jack.</u>

8. Look and complete.

Brazil   'm   from   They're

1. She's from _____.

2. I_____ from Japan.

3. _____ from Argentina.

4. He's _____ Italy.

9. Write the questions.

What's _____ _____

How _____ _____

Where _____ _____

Can you _____ _____

My name's Ken.

I'm eleven years old.

I'm from Japan.

Yes, I can speak English and Japanese.

10. Read and complete.

| Italian | from | Spain | 10 | speak | English |

Hi! My name's Patricia

and I'm from _____ .

I'm _____ years old. I _____

Spanish and _____ .

This is my friend Giorgio.

He's _____ Italy.

He's _____ .

11. Read. Then circle the correct sentence.

1. I from Italy.   I'm from Italy.

2. They speaks Spanish.   They speak Spanish.

3. She's Brazilian.   She's Brazil.

4. He speaks Japanese.   He speaks Japan.

12. Ask your friends and write.

	Friend 1	Friend 2
Name:		
Age:		
Nationality:		
Languages:		

Now I know

- ☐ Where are you from?
- ☐ I'm from Japan. I'm Japanese.
- ☐ ... is Spanish. ... lives in Spain.
- ☐ ... is eleven years old.
- ☐ ... speaks Greek/Spanish/English.

Unit 2 Fast, faster ...

1. Find and write.

bigger   slower   faster

big _____   fast _____   slow _____

2. Look and write.

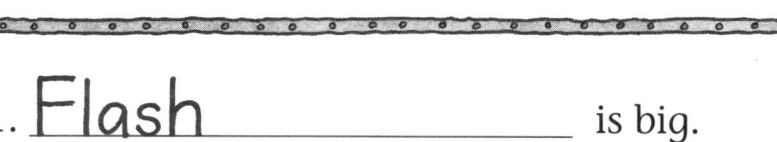

1. Flash _____ is big.

_____ is bigger.

2. _____ is fast.

_____ is faster.

3. _____ is slow.

_____ is slower.

3. Complete and answer.

It's shorter than the 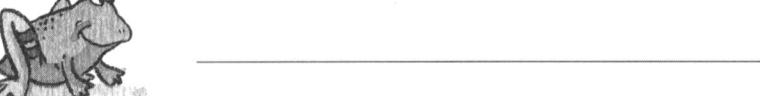 _____.

It's smaller than the  _____.

It's slower than the 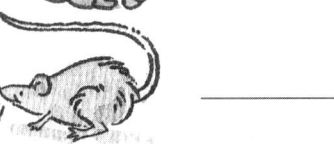 _____.

What is it? _____.

4. Write about the animals.

1. giraffe/camel   taller

   The giraffe is taller than the _____

2. horse/tortoise   faster

   _____

3. mouse/rabbit   smaller

   _____

4. elephant/zebra   bigger

   _____

5. snail/lion   slower

   _____

6. frog/penguin   shorter

   _____

5. Look, read and complete.

I'm _____ centimetres tall.

_____ is 141 centimetres tall.

Leo is 145 _____ tall.

Sam is _____ centimetres tall.

And _____ is

78 centimetres _____.

6. Read and answer. USE WORKBOOK PAGE 11.

1. Is Jane shorter than Ken?

   <u>No, she isn't.</u>

2. Is Leo taller than Sam?

   _____

3. Is Ken shorter than Sam?

   _____

4. Is Jane taller than Sam and Leo?

   _____

5. Is Leo shorter than Sam and Ken?

   _____

6. Is Bonbon taller than the rabbit?

   _____

7. Read and complete. USE WORKBOOK PAGE 11.

Maria is <u>133</u> centimetres tall.

She is _____ than

Bonbon, _____ and

_____ .

But she is _____

than _____ ,

_____

and _____ .

8. Write.

1. big **bigger** _____

2. _____ stronger

3. fast _____

4. _____ older

5. young _____

6. _____ slower

9. Look and write.

faster	older	~~taller~~	stronger

1. I'm

taller _____

than you.

3. I'm

_____

than you.

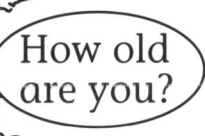

How old are you?

2. I'm

_____

than you.

4. I'm

_____

than you.

10. Write smaller than/bigger than.

1. The penguin is _____ the rabbit.

2. The zebra is _____ the elephant.

3. The elephant is _____ the camel.

4. The snail is _____ the frog.

11. Write questions and ask your friends.

USE PUPIL'S BOOK PAGE 18.

Is the

Is the snail longer than the snake?

No, it isn't.

12. Find out and complete the chart.

How tall are you and your friends?

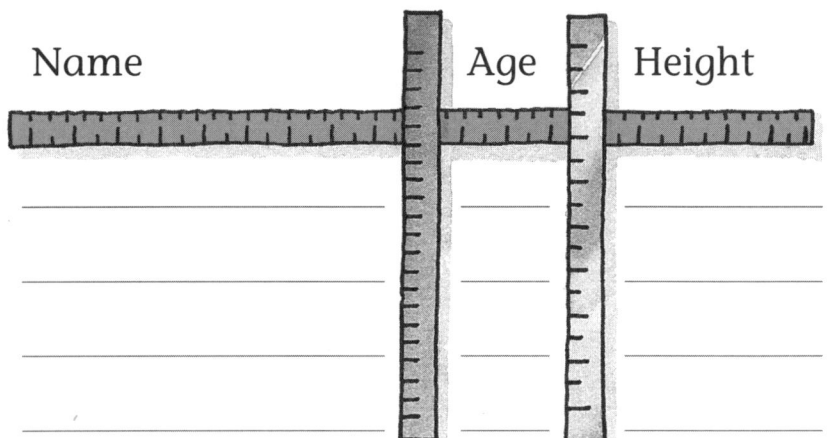

Name	Age	Height

Now write about your friends.

I'm _____ than _____

_____

_____

Now I know

- ☐ The ... is bigger than the ... .
- ☐ Is ... taller/shorter/longer than ... ?
- ☐ Yes, he/she/it is. No, he/she/it isn't.
- ☐ I'm/He/She/It is ... centimetres tall.
- ☐ I'm taller than ... .
- ☐ But I'm shorter than ... .

Unit 2

Where's the school?

1. Find and write.

school	supermarket	hospital	bank

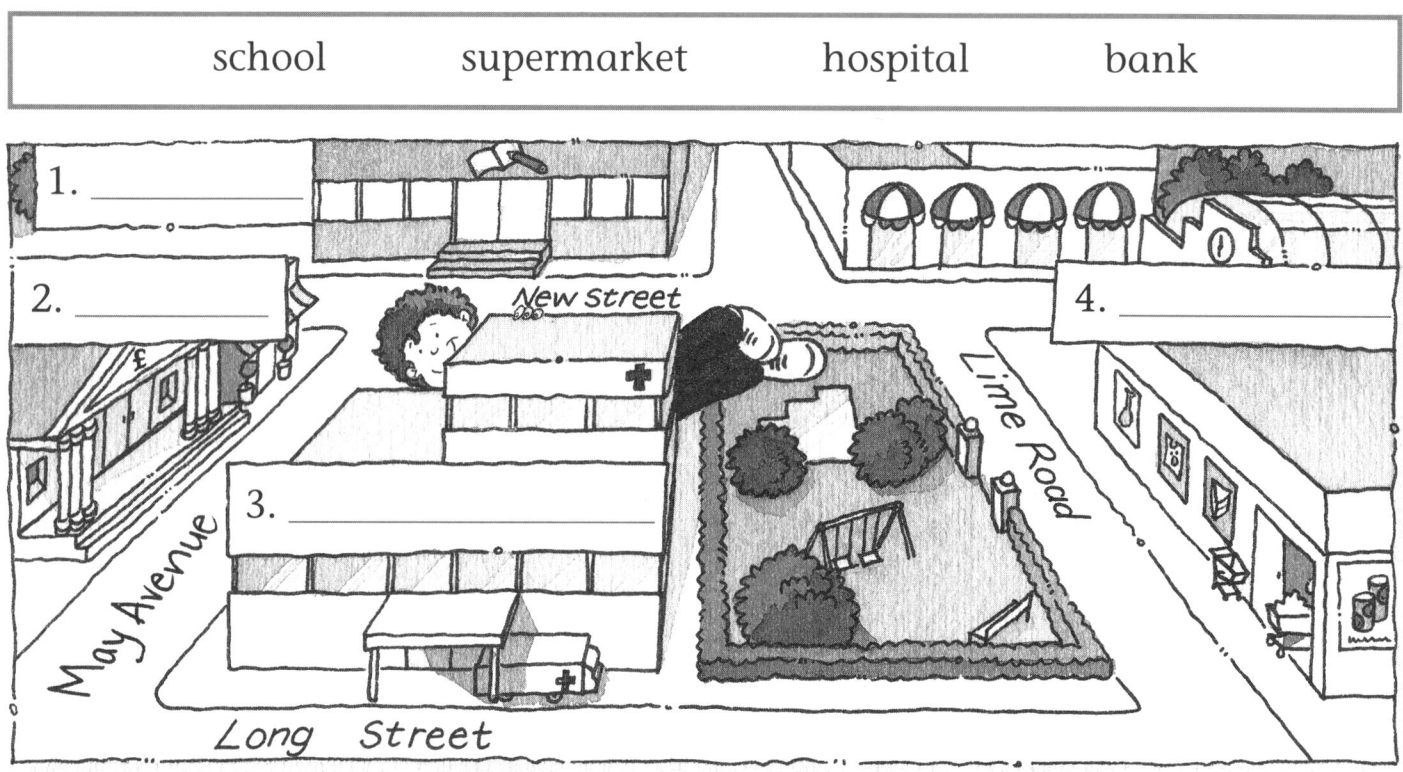

1. _____

2. _____

3. _____

4. _____

2. Complete and answer.

1. The _____ is in May Avenue.

2. The _____ is in Long S_____

3. The _____ is in Lime _____

4. The _____ is in _____

5. And where's Toby? He's in _____

3. Read and write the places on the map.

Where's the park?	It's in Green Street.
Where's the bakery?	It's in Elm Avenue.
Where's the train station?	It's in Station Road.

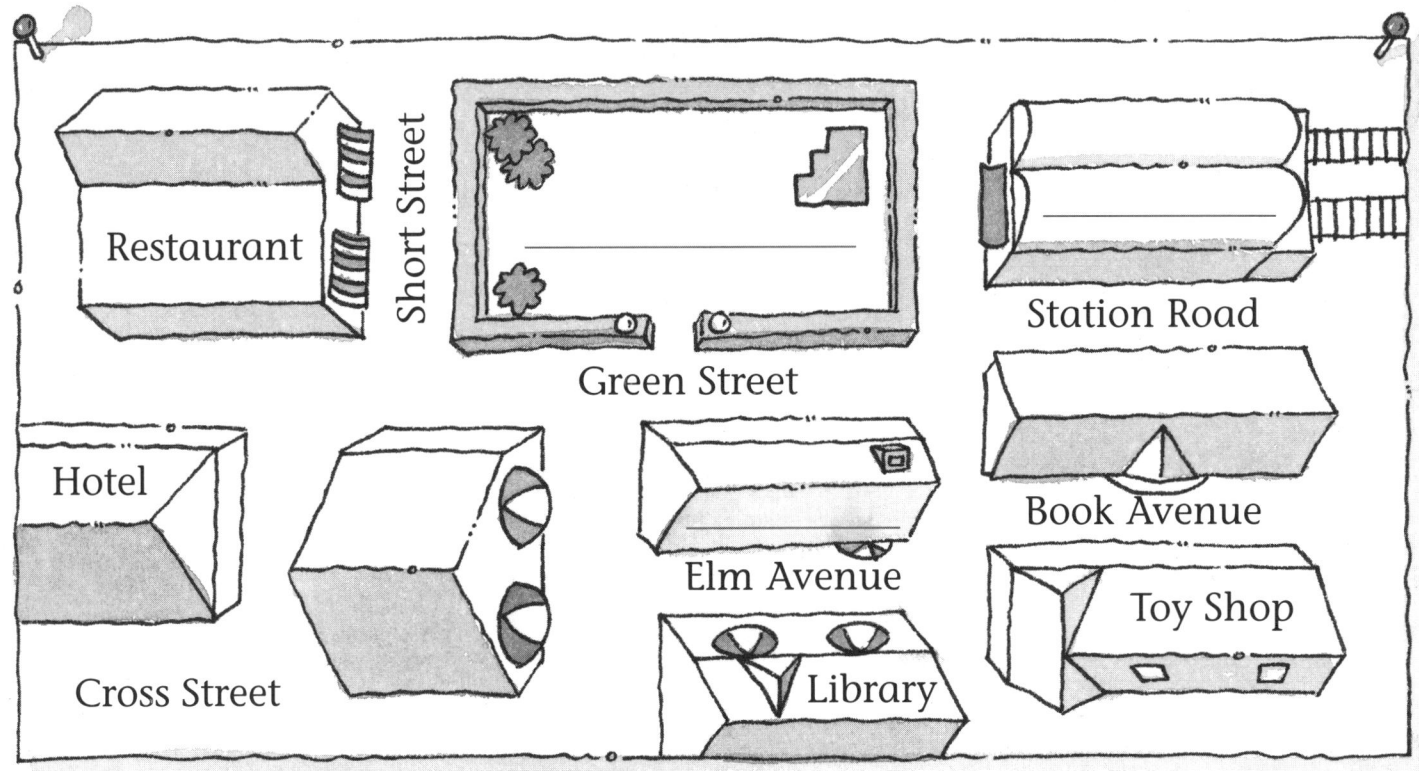

4. Complete the questions and answer.

1. Where's the toy shop?

It's in _____

2. _____ the library?

_____

3. _____ hotel?

_____

4. _____ restaurant?

_____

5. Find and write.

| behind | between | ~~next to~~ | in front of | opposite |

    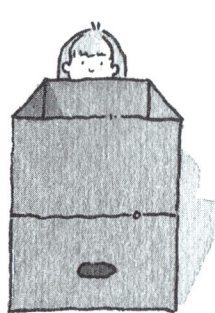

next to _____ _____ _____ _____

6. Look and complete.

1. Toby is _____ Ken.

2. Ken is _____

   Anna and Toby.

3. Anna is _____

   Bonbon.

4. _____ is

   _____ Anna.

7. Look, read and answer True or False.

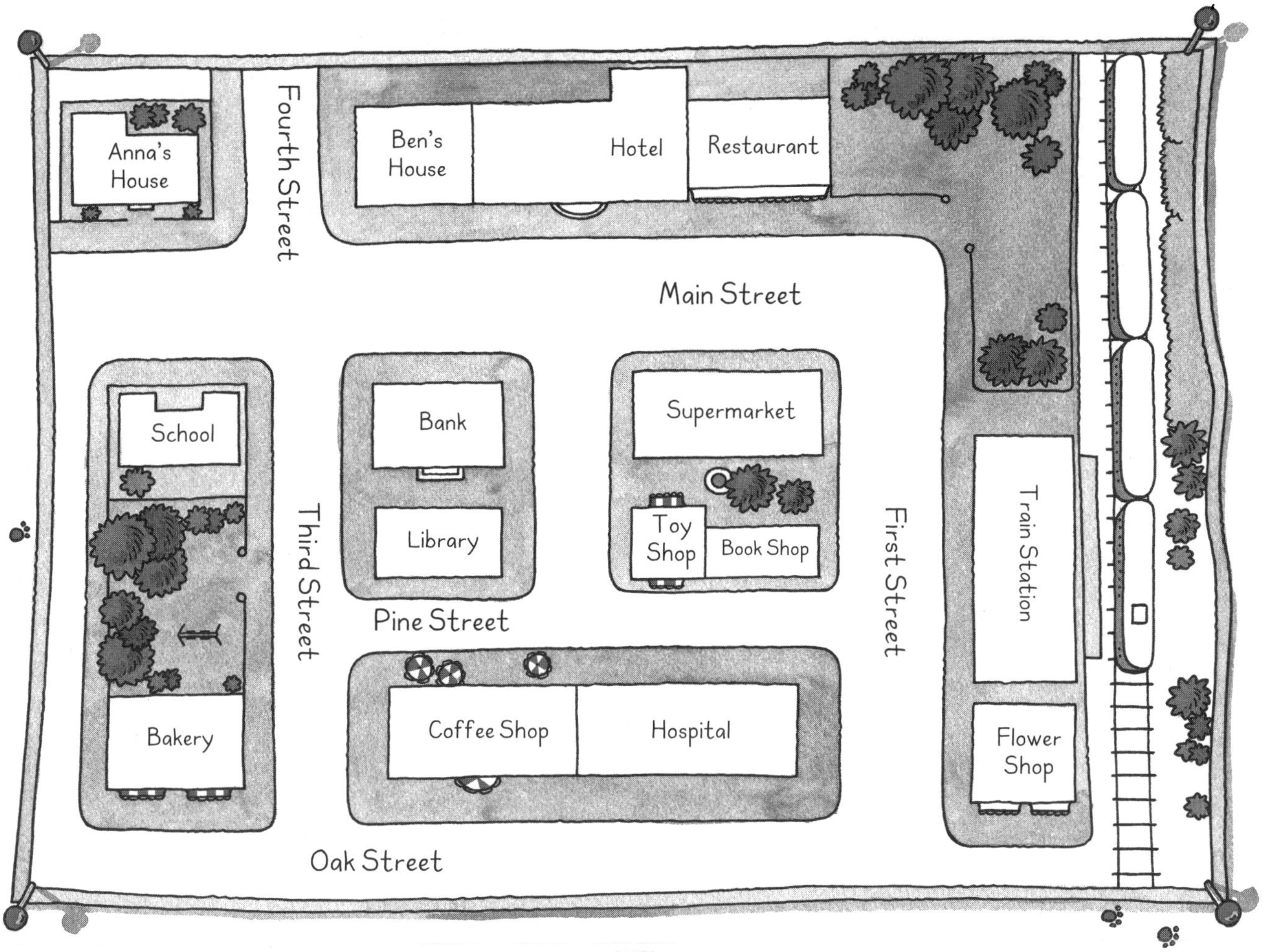

1. The library is in front of the bank. _True_

2. The hospital is behind the coffee shop. _____

3. The supermarket is next to the book shop. _____

4. The hotel is next to the restaurant. _____

5. The bakery is between the school and the park. _____

8. Correct the false sentences.

1. _____

2. _____

3. _____

9. Look and write.

1. <u>Hospital</u>   4. _____   7. _____

2. _____   5. _____   8. _____

3. _____   6. _____   9. _____

                                                        10. _____

10. Match.

teacher   restaurant

baker   school

doctor   hospital

waiter   supermarket

shop assistant   bakery

11. Write sentences.

1. <u>A teacher works in a school.</u>

2. _____

3. _____

4. _____

5. _____

12. Look and write.

1. Bonbon is <u>in front of</u> the trees.

2. Bonbon is _____ the trees.

3. Bonbon ____ _____ _____ trees.

4. Bonbon ____ _____ ____ ____ _____

5. _____ ___ _____ ____ _____

13. Draw a map and write about your house.

Where's your house? My house is _____

_____

_____

_____

Now I know

- [ ] Where's the ... ?
- [ ] It's on ... Road/Street/Avenue.
- [ ] It's next to/behind/between/ in front of the ... /opposite.
- [ ] A teacher works in a ... .
- [ ] I'm/He's/She's a doctor.

Don't feed the animals.

1. Find and write the number.

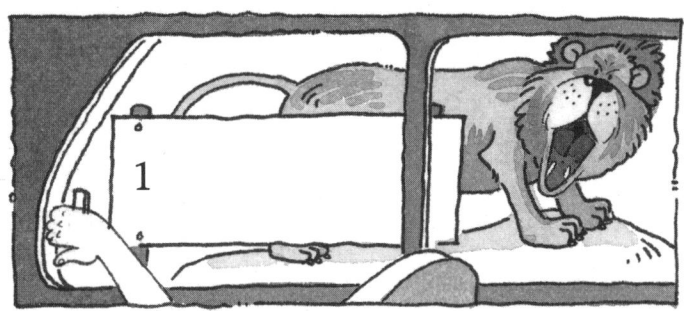

Touch the fish gently. ☐		Don't feed the animals. ☐	
Don't shout. ☐		Don't open the window. ☐	

2. Look and write.

1. Don't _____
_____

3. _____
_____

2. _____
_____

4. _____
_____

3. Choose and write.

Don't walk on the grass.	Eat here.	Don't run.

1. _____
   _____

2. _____
   _____

3. _____
   _____

4. Draw and write.

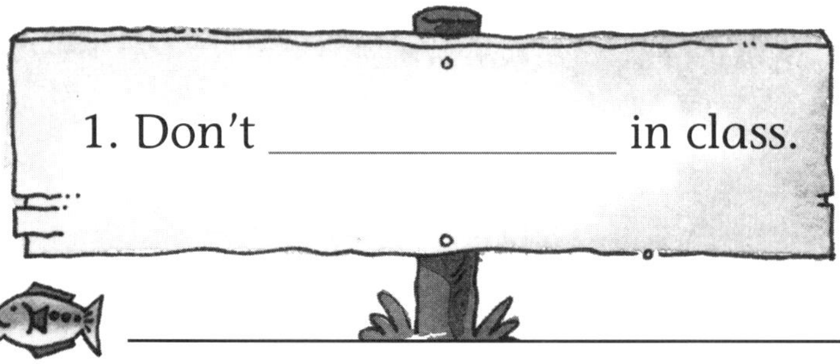

1. Don't _____ in class.

2. _____ to the teacher.

5. Answer True or False.

In the sun.

Put on sunscreen. _____

Don't wear a hat. _____

At school.

Don't drop litter. _____

Eat in class. _____

At home.

Don't tidy your bedroom. _____

Eat your breakfast. _____

6. Correct the false sentences.

1. _____

2. _____

3. _____

7. Choose and write the rules.

Don't	Make open Put wear Drink Go run	a the on

It's snowing.

1. _____
_____ window.

2. _____
_____ hat.

3. _____
_____ snowman.

4. _____
_____ the ice.

It's hot.

5. _____
_____ water.

6. _____
_____ jumper.

7. _____
_____ sunscreen.

8. _____
_____ swimming.

8. Read and draw.

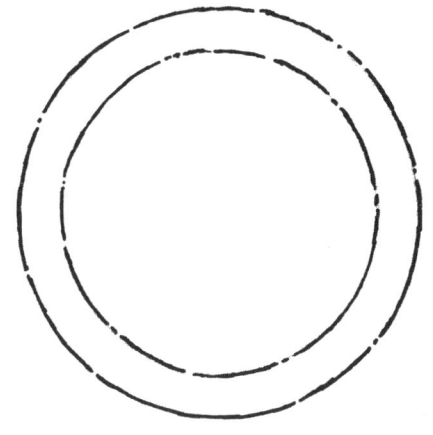

1. Don't swim!

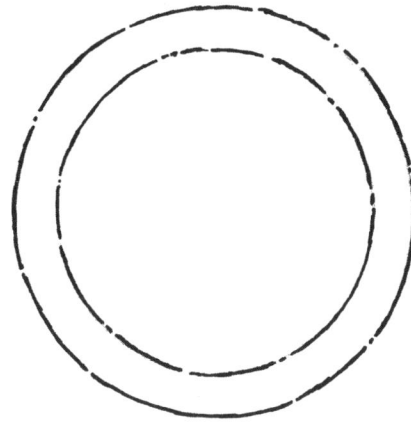

2. Don't talk!

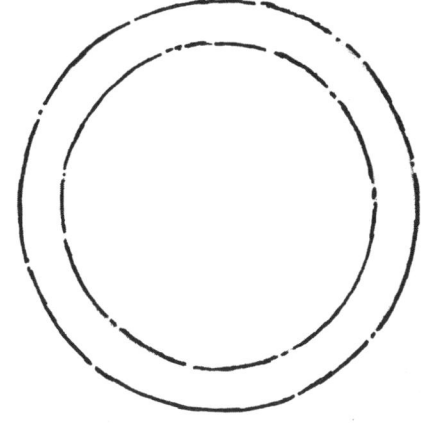

3. Don't touch!

9. Write me/it/her/him/them.

1. Give  to

<u>Give it to him.</u>

4. Don't feed

_____.

2. Give  to

_____.

5. Give 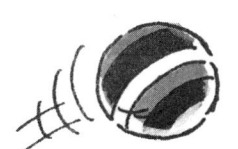 to

_____.

3. Feed

_____.

10. Match.

a. Make your bed. __2__

b. Close the door. _____

c. Don't eat in bed. _____

d. Pick up your socks. _____

e. Do your homework. _____

f. Tidy your desk. _____

11. Now complete the note.

Make your bed.

_____ _____ your socks.

_____ your homework.

_____ your desk.

_____ the door.

_____ _____ in bed.

Thank you!

Mum.

12. Complete the key with pictures. Then draw and ask your friends to write.

Key

Don't

open

touch

the

animals

door

fish

run

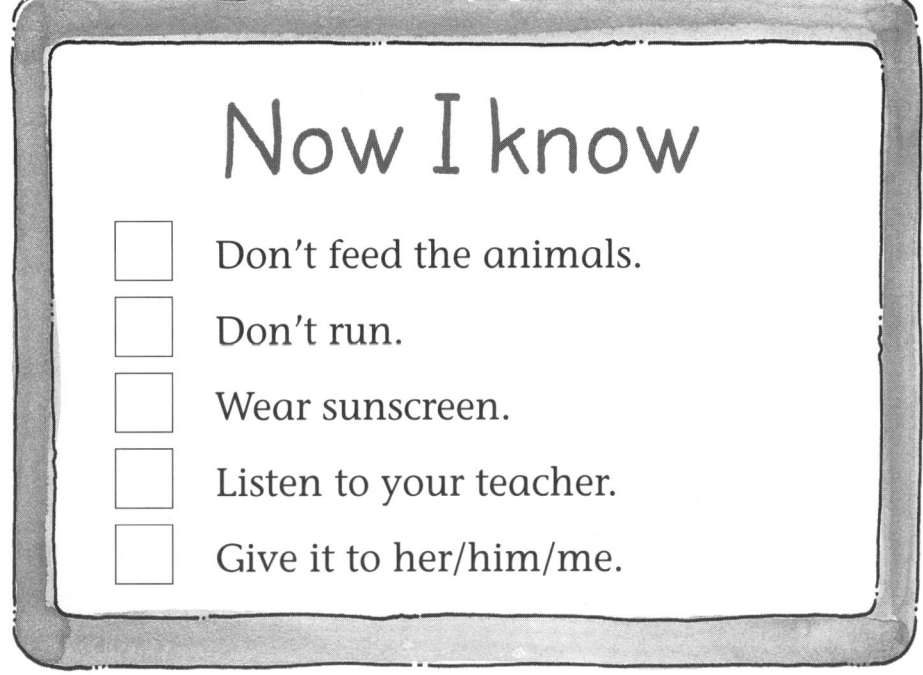

1. Don't touch the animals.

2. _____

3. _____

4. _____

Now I know

☐ Don't feed the animals.

☐ Don't run.

☐ Wear sunscreen.

☐ Listen to your teacher.

☐ Give it to her/him/me.

Were you at the beach?

1. Find and write.

| fair | lake | beach |

1. I was at the _____

2. I was at the _____

3. I was at the _____

2. Look and write.

Were you at the beach yesterday?

1. No, I wasn't. I was at the _____

2. _____

3. _____

3. Look and write.

1. <u>I was at</u>   2. _____   3. _____

_____   _____   _____

4. Look and write the questions.

1. <u>Were you at the beach</u>
<u>yesterday?</u>

No, I wasn't.

2. <u>Were</u> _____

_____

Yes, I was.

3. _____

_____

Yes, I was.

4. _____

_____

Yes, I was.

5. Look at the pictures. Complete the story.

Tortoise was faster than Hare.   She was slow.
Soon Hare was asleep.   Yesterday Hare and Tortoise were at the park.

Yesterday

Tortoise was tired.

Hare: I'm bored. I want a race.
Tortoise: Go away, I'm tired.
Hare: I'm faster than you.
Tortoise: OK. Let's race.

Hare: Ready?
Tortoise: Ready.
Hare: Go.
Hare was very fast. Tortoise wasn't fast. _____

Hare was hot and thirsty.
Hare: I want some ice cream and a drink.
Then Hare was tired.
Hare: Oh, I'm tired.

_____

Tortoise: Look, there's Hare. He's asleep.

Hare: Stop!
But it was too late.

_____

Tortoise: You were slow, Hare. So, I'm the winner!

6. Read the story again and correct the sentences.

1. Hare and Tortoise weren't at the park.

<u>Hare and Tortoise were at the park.</u>

2. Tortoise was bored.

_____

3. Hare was hot and hungry.

_____

4. Hare wasn't asleep.

_____

5. Hare was faster than Tortoise.

_____

6. Hare was the winner.

7. Write was or were.

I _____   It _____

You _____   We _____

He _____   You _____

She _____   They _____

8. Write was or were and complete.

1. Freddy __was__ at the  _beach._

2. My mum and dad _____ at the  _____

3. My sister and I _____ at  _____

4. My dad _____ at the  _____

5. The boy _____ at the  _____

6. Kate _____ in the  _____

9. Write he/she/it/we/they.

Toby = <u>he</u>   My mum = _____   My mum and dad =

Kate = _____   My dad = _____   _____

The boy = _____   My sister = _____   The children =

The girl = _____   My sister and I =   _____

The cat = _____   _____   My friends =

The dog = _____   My brother = _____   _____

Kate, Toby and Ben =   My brother and I =   The cat and dog =

_____   _____   _____

10. Write Yes, he was/No, he wasn't/ Yes, she was/No, she wasn't.

1. Was Maria at the beach? <u>No, she wasn't.</u>

2. Was Anna at the lake? _____

3. Was Smile at the beach? _____

4. Was Toby at home? _____

11. Ask your friends and write ✓ or ✗.

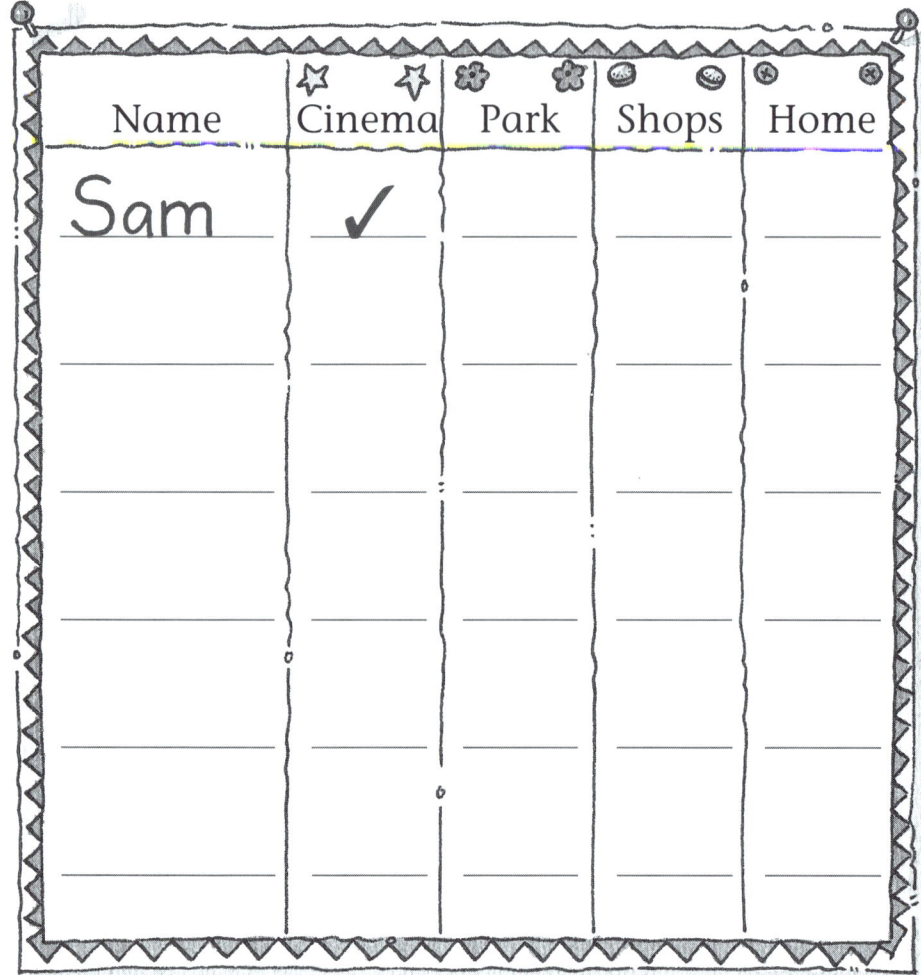

Name	Cinema	Park	Shops	Home
Sam	✓			

Were you at the cinema on Saturday?

Yes, I was.

Now I know

- ☐ Were you at the beach yesterday?
- ☐ Yes, I was./No, I wasn't.
- ☐ I/You/He/She/It was/wasn't ... .
- ☐ We/You/They were/weren't ... .

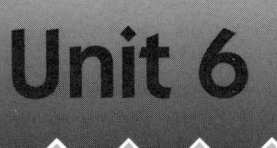

I played baseball.

1. Read and write the names.

I played baseball.
Maria

I collected shells.
Anna

I sailed a boat.
Ken

We climbed a tree.
Toby and Bonbon

2. Look, read and complete.

Yesterday Maria played _____

_____.

Ken ____ ____ ____ _____.

Anna _____ _____

and Toby and Bonbon _____

_____ _____.

3. Write.

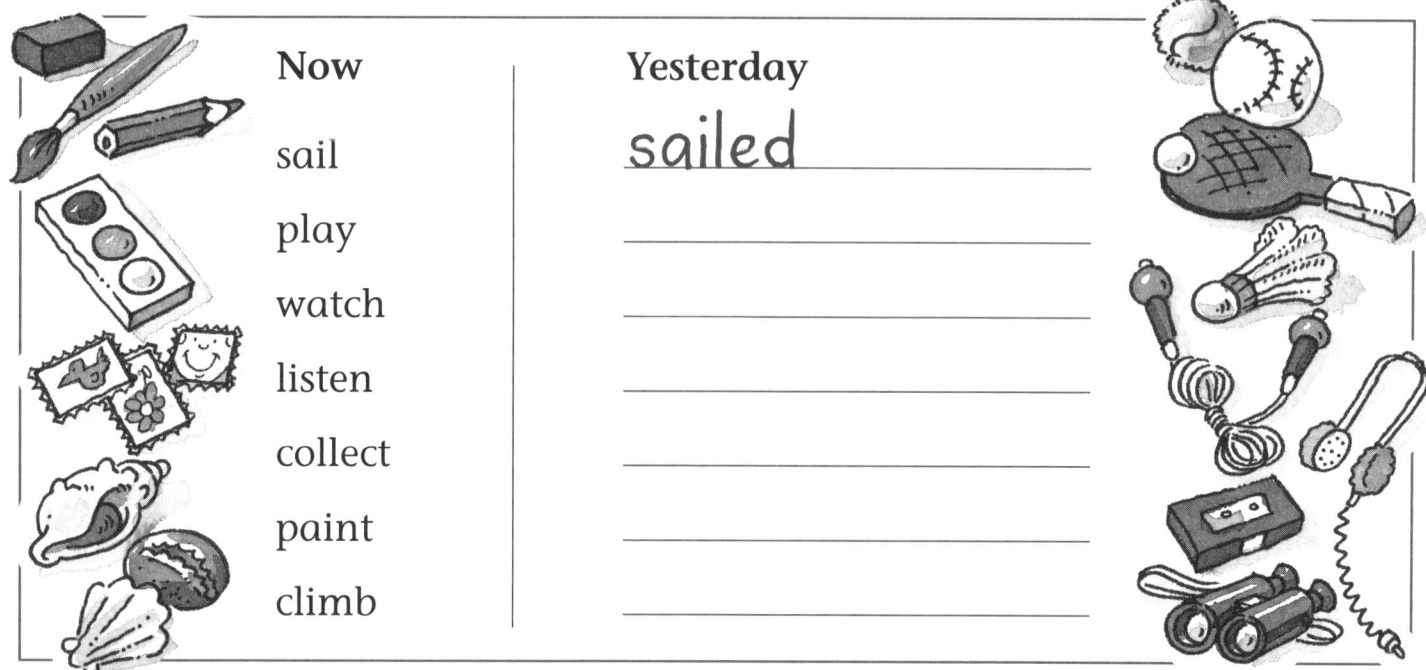

Now	Yesterday
sail	sailed
play	
watch	
listen	
collect	
paint	
climb	

4. Look and write.

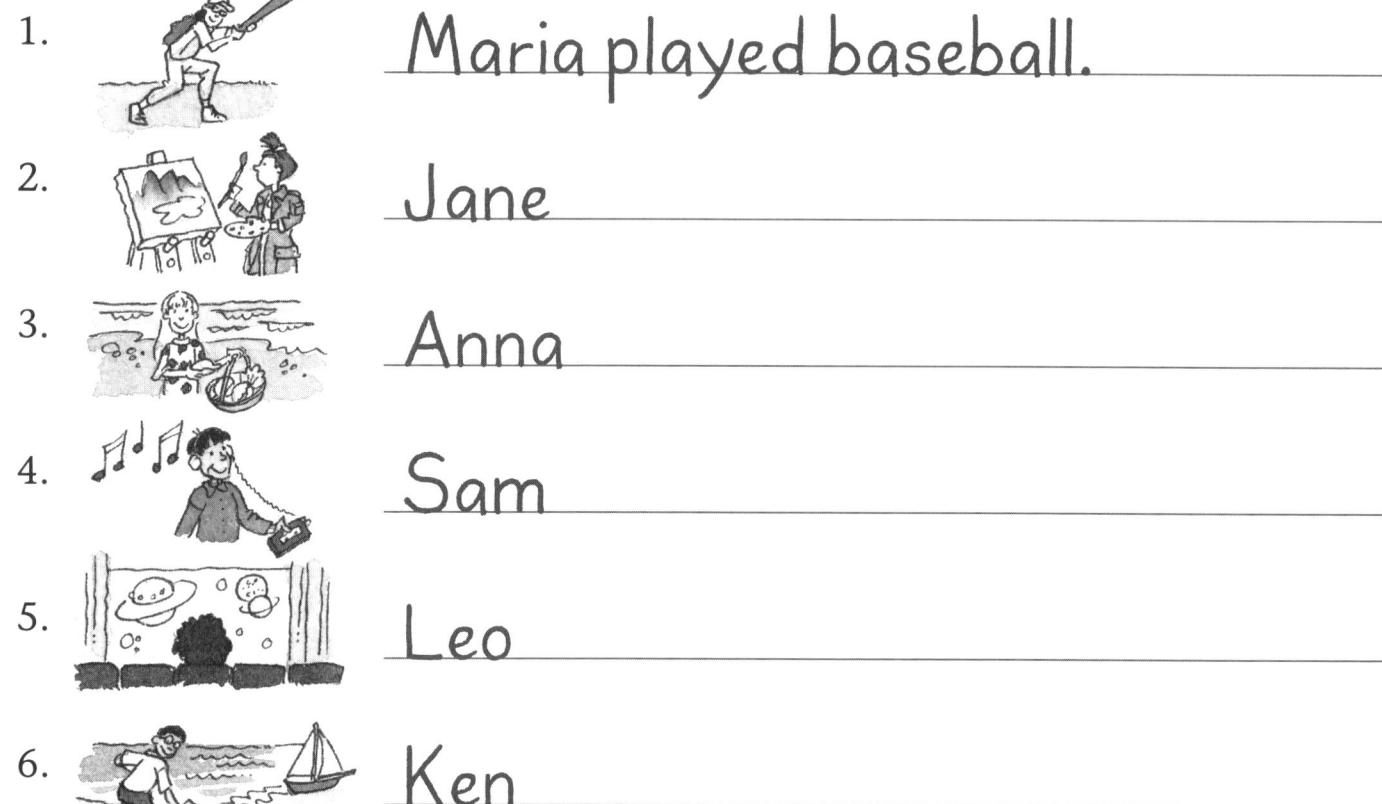

1. Maria played baseball.

2. Jane

3. Anna

4. Sam

5. Leo

6. Ken

5. Sort and write.

1. played/On/I/Monday/baseball.

   <u>On Monday I</u> _____

2. Tuesday/I/shells/the/collected/beach./at/On

   _____

3. I/town./to/walked/On/Wednesday

   _____

4. a/film./watched/I/Thursday/On

   _____

5. Friday/On/the/I/visited/museum.

   _____

6. Complete Leo's diary.

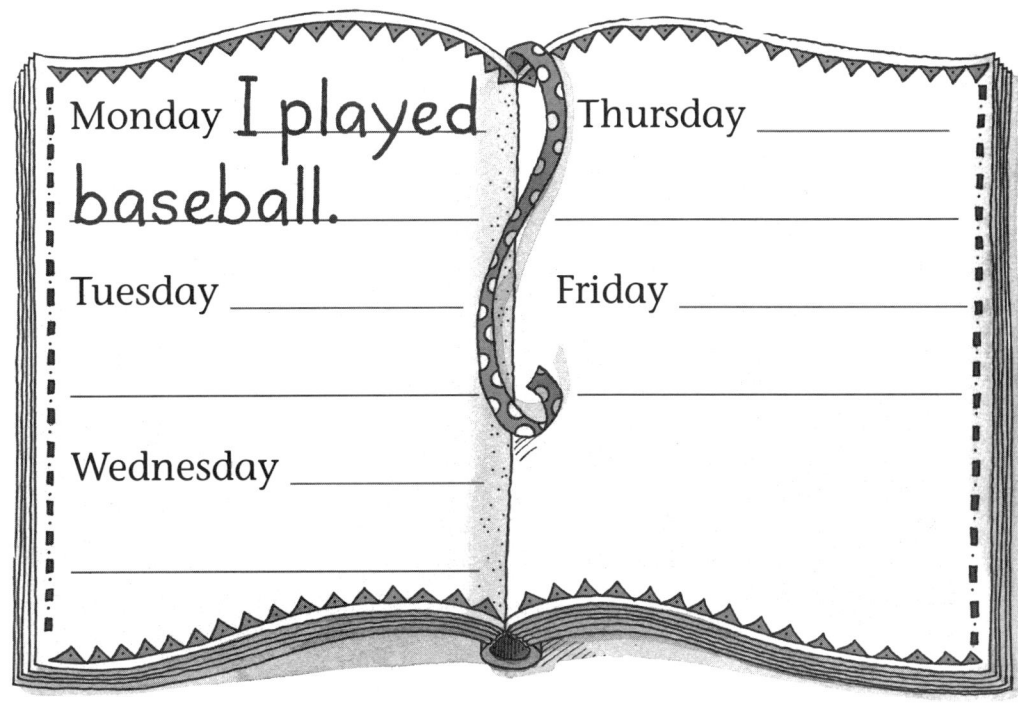

Monday <u>I played baseball.</u>

Tuesday _____

Wednesday _____

Thursday _____

Friday _____

7. Look and write.

1 Monday/rained   to music

On Monday it rained.
Kate listened to music.

2 Tuesday/was cloudy   to the fair

3 Wednesday/was sunny   at the beach

4 Thursday/was cold and windy   computer games

5 Friday/rained   a picture

8. Look and answer.

Monday	Tuesday	Wednesday	Thursday	Friday

1. What did Toby do on Wednesday? He listened to music.

2. What did Toby do on Friday? _____

3. What did Toby do on Tuesday? _____

4. What did Toby do on Monday? _____

5. What did Toby do on Thursday? _____

9. Complete the questions. Then answer Yes, I did/No, I didn't.

1. Toby, did you listen to music on Friday? No, I didn't.

2. Toby, _____ you sail a boat on Monday? _____

3. Toby, _____ you _____ basketball on Tuesday?

   _____

4. Toby, _____ _____ _____ a film on Thursday?

   _____

5. Toby, _____ _____ _____ a picture on Wednesday?

   _____

10. Look and complete.

1. I didn't sail a boat.

2. I didn't _____ a film.

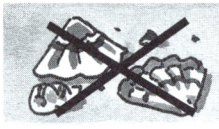
3. I _____ _____ shells.

4. ____ _____ _____ ____ picture.

5. ____ _____ _____ _____.

11. Write and draw what you did yesterday.

Yesterday, I _____

_____

_____

12. Read and complete. USE PUPIL'S BOOK PAGE 50.

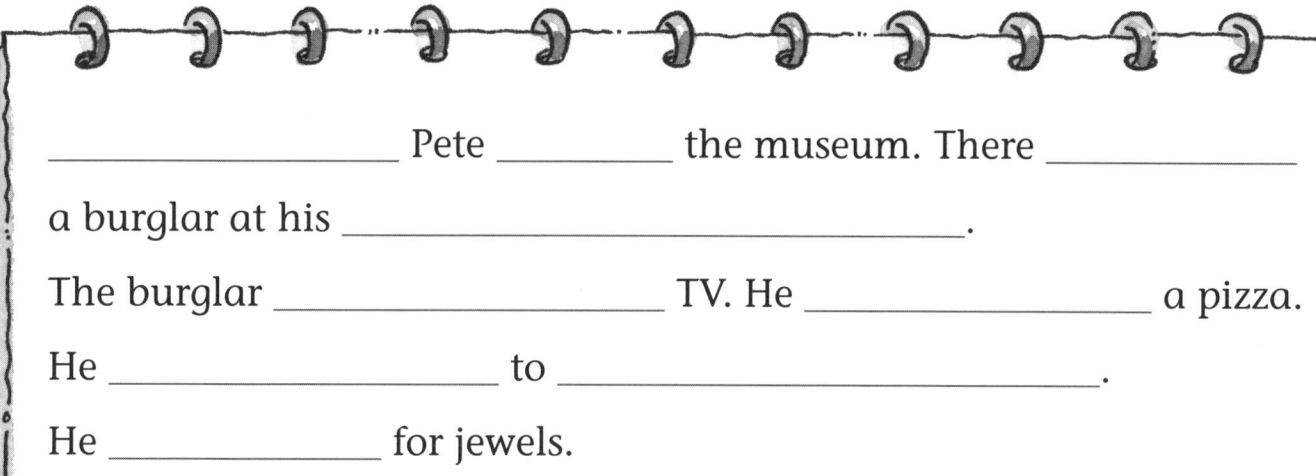

_____ Pete _____ the museum. There _____ a burglar at his _____.

The burglar _____ TV. He _____ a pizza.

He _____ to _____.

He _____ for jewels.

He _____ out of _____ _____.

A _____ officer _____ outside.

Now I know

- ☐ Yesterday I played volleyball.
- ☐ He/She listened to music.
- ☐ He/She watched TV.
- ☐ What did X do yesterday?
- ☐ I/You/He/She didn't play basketball.

Treasure Hunt

1. Find and write.

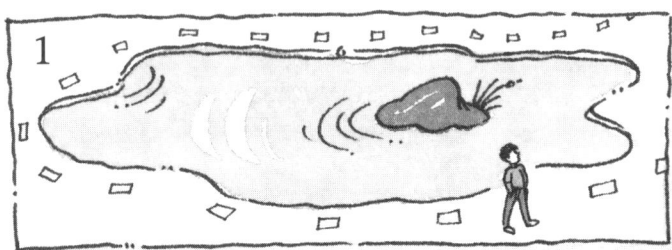
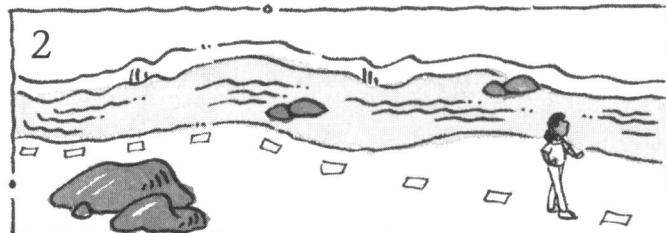

along the river ☐   through the forest ☐   around the lake ☐

2. Look and write.

Anna and Sam went on a  _____

hunt yesterday. They went around the  _____ and

along the  _____. Then they went through the

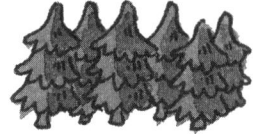 _____. The  _____

was under a 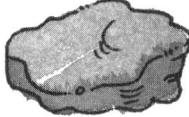 _____.

3. Look and write.

1. <u>along the river</u>   2. _____   3. _____   4. _____

4. Look and write.

<u>Leo went around the lake</u>   <u>Kate _____</u>

_____   _____

_____   _____

_____   _____

5. Read and draw the path.

First we went around **Green Lake**. Then we went along the river and over **Fish Bridge**. Next we went over **Snake Mountain** and through **Happy Forest**. Then we walked along the beach. The treasure was under **Bird Mountain**.

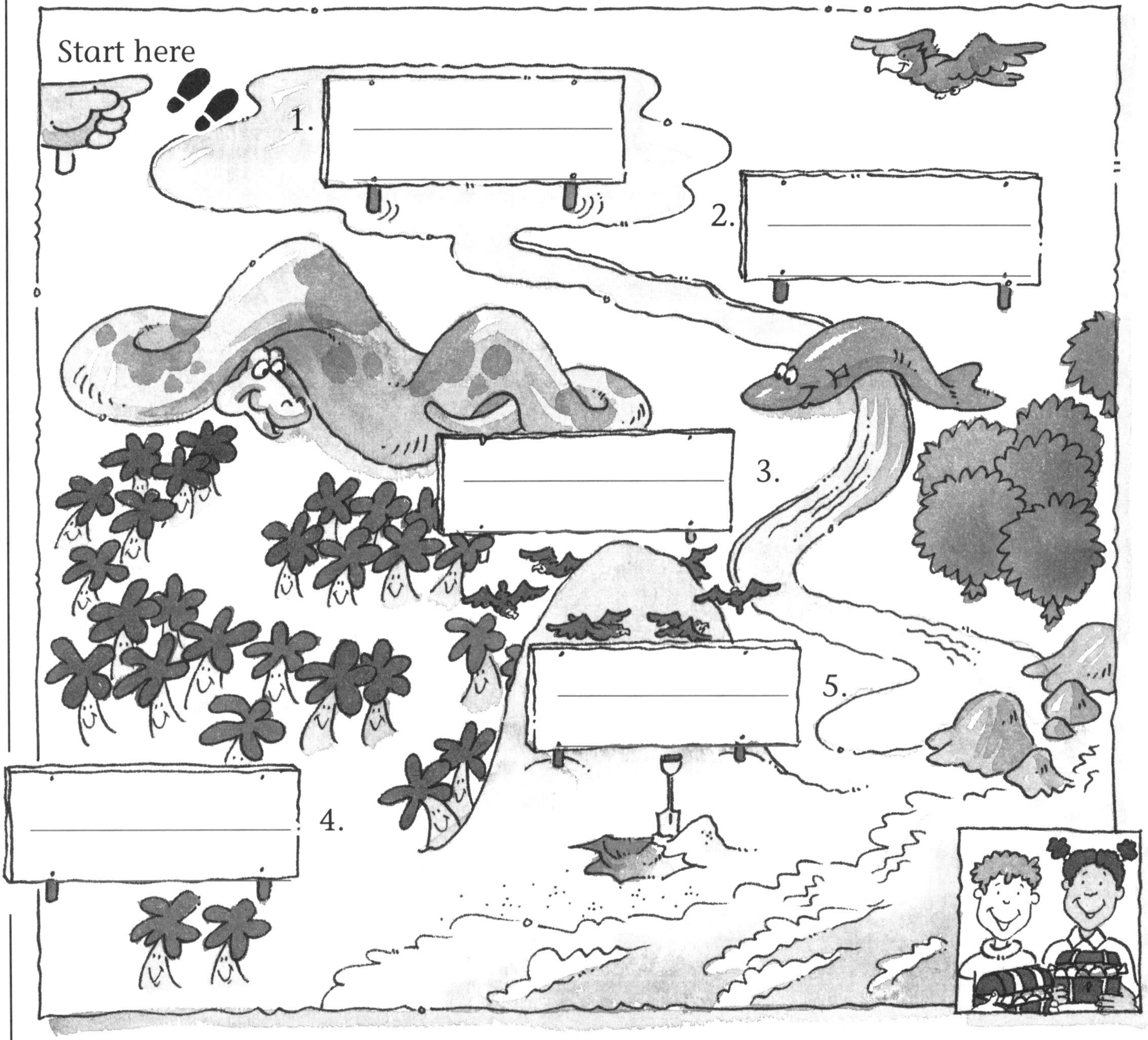

Start here

1. _____

2. _____

3.

4. _____

5.

Now write the names of the places on the signposts.

6. Draw the pictures on the map. Then with a friend ask and answer.

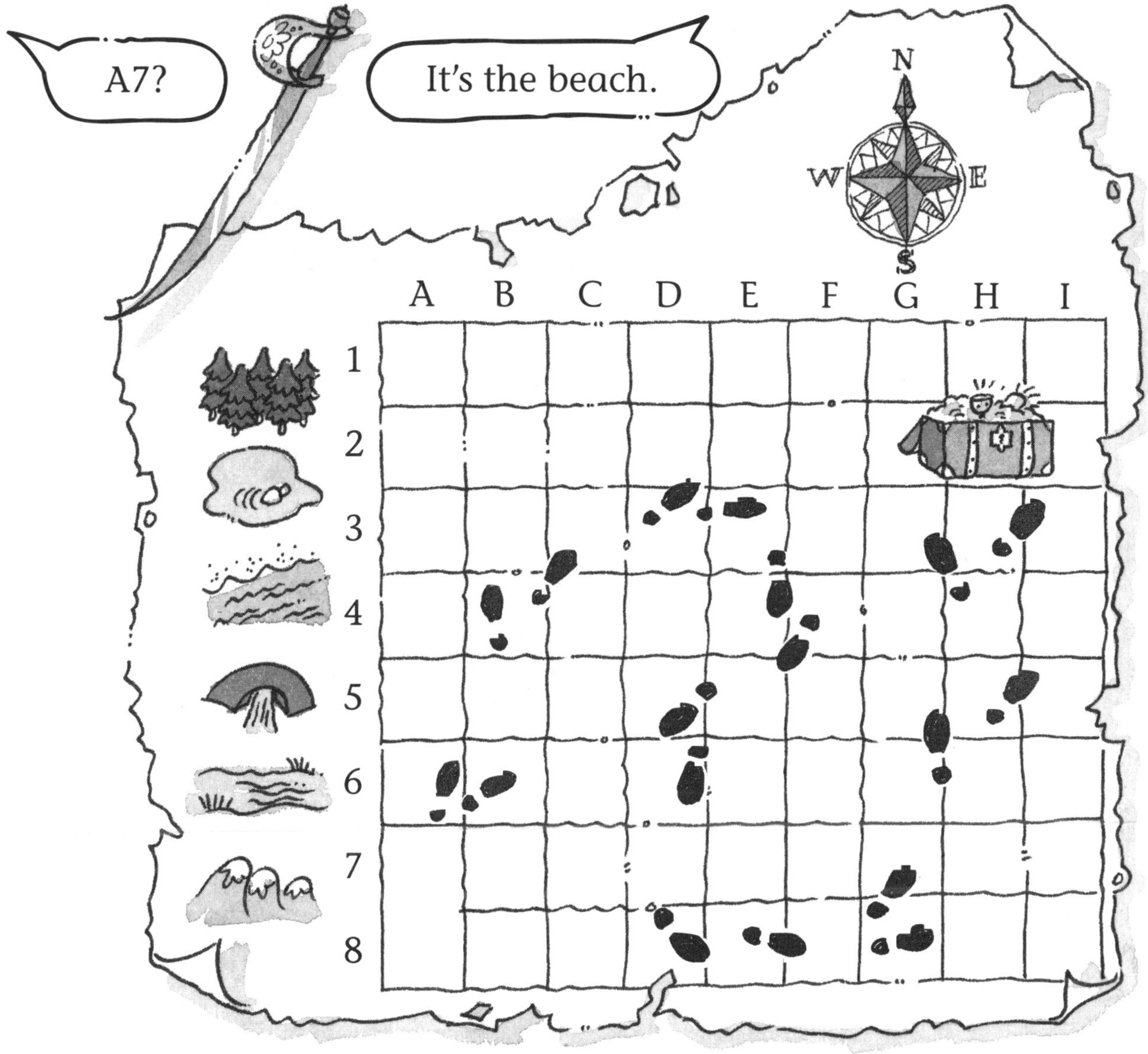

A7?

It's the beach.

	A	B	C	D	E	F	G	H	I
1									
2									
3									
4									
5									
6									
7									
8									

7. Look and write.

Where did you go? First I went _____

_____

Where was the treasure? _____

_____

8. Write didn't go and complete.

1. I __didn't go__ to the cinema.
   I __went__ to the museum.

2. I _____ _____ to the _____. I _____ to the fair.

3. I _____ _____ to _____ _____. I _____ to the _____.

4. I _____ _____ _____ _____. I _____ _____ the _____.

9. Write the questions.

1. you/fair? __Did you go to the fair?__

2. he/beach? _____

3. she/museum? _____

4. Toby/library? _____

5. Kate and Anna/cinema? _____

6. Leo and Ken/lake? _____

10. Look and answer.

This is Jake.   This is Bob.

1. Did Bob go under the bridge? No, he didn't.

2. Did Bob go through the forest? _____

3. Did Bob go along the river? _____

4. Did Bob go over the mountains? _____

5. Did Jake go over the bridge? _____

6. Did Jake go around the forest? _____

7. Did Jake go along the river? _____

8. Did Jake go over the mountains? _____

11. Look, read and correct.

First I went through the forest. Next I went over Black mountain. Then I went along the river. I buried the treasure in the forest.

Now I know

- ☐ Where did X go?
- ☐ X went over/around/ along/through the … .
- ☐ Did you go … ? Did X go to the … ? Yes, I/he/she did./No, I/he/she didn't.
- ☐ I didn't go … .
- ☐ I/We/They went … .

Christmas

1. Write.

My Christmas list

2. Look at your list and draw presents under the tree.

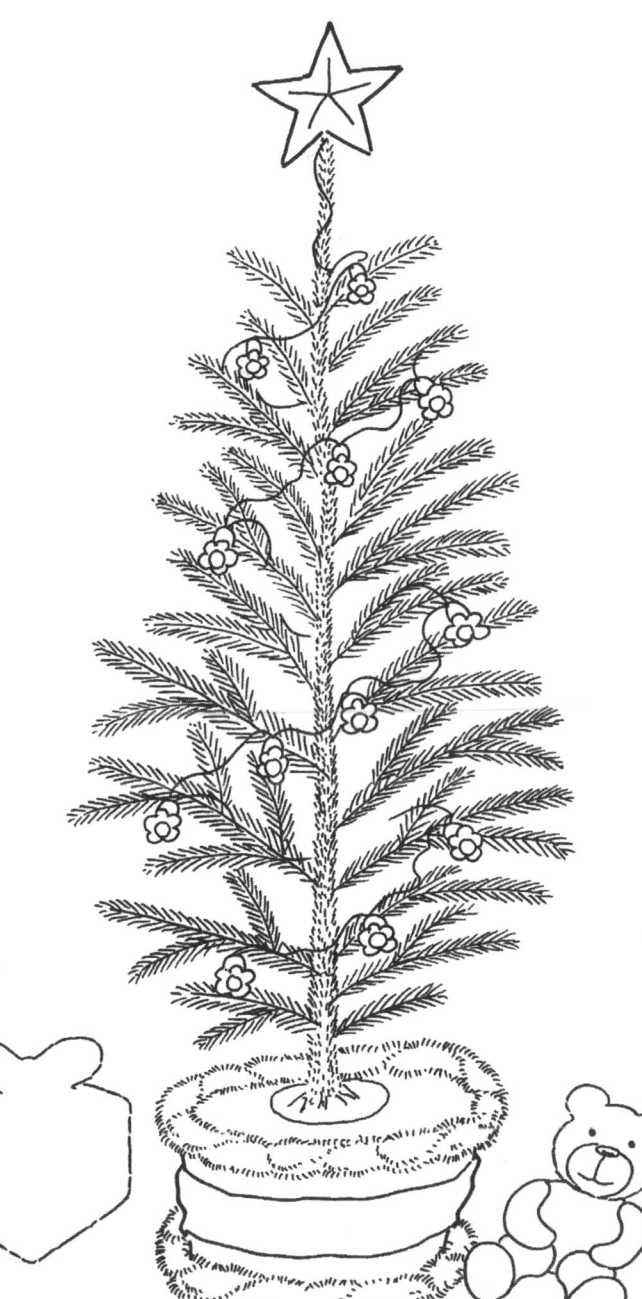

3. Read and colour.

1. Father Christmas is wearing a red hat, black shoes and a red and white jacket.
2. Maria is wearing a blue and yellow hat.
3. The dog is brown and white.
4. Three presents are green and one present is orange.
5. The streamers are yellow, pink and grey.

4. Find and write.

Find two things beginning with t. _____ _____

Find two things beginning with c. _____ _____

Find two things beginning with s. _____ _____

Valentine's Day

1. Complete the message in the card for your friend. Then colour.

Valentine   Love   Kisses

To _____

Be my _____

_____ and _____

From   ?

2. Complete the sentences.

1. Valentine's Day is on _____ of _____

2. People send each other _____

3. People give each other _____

Picture Dictionary

Cut out the pictures on pages 57 and 59.
Stick them in the right place here to make
your picture dictionary.

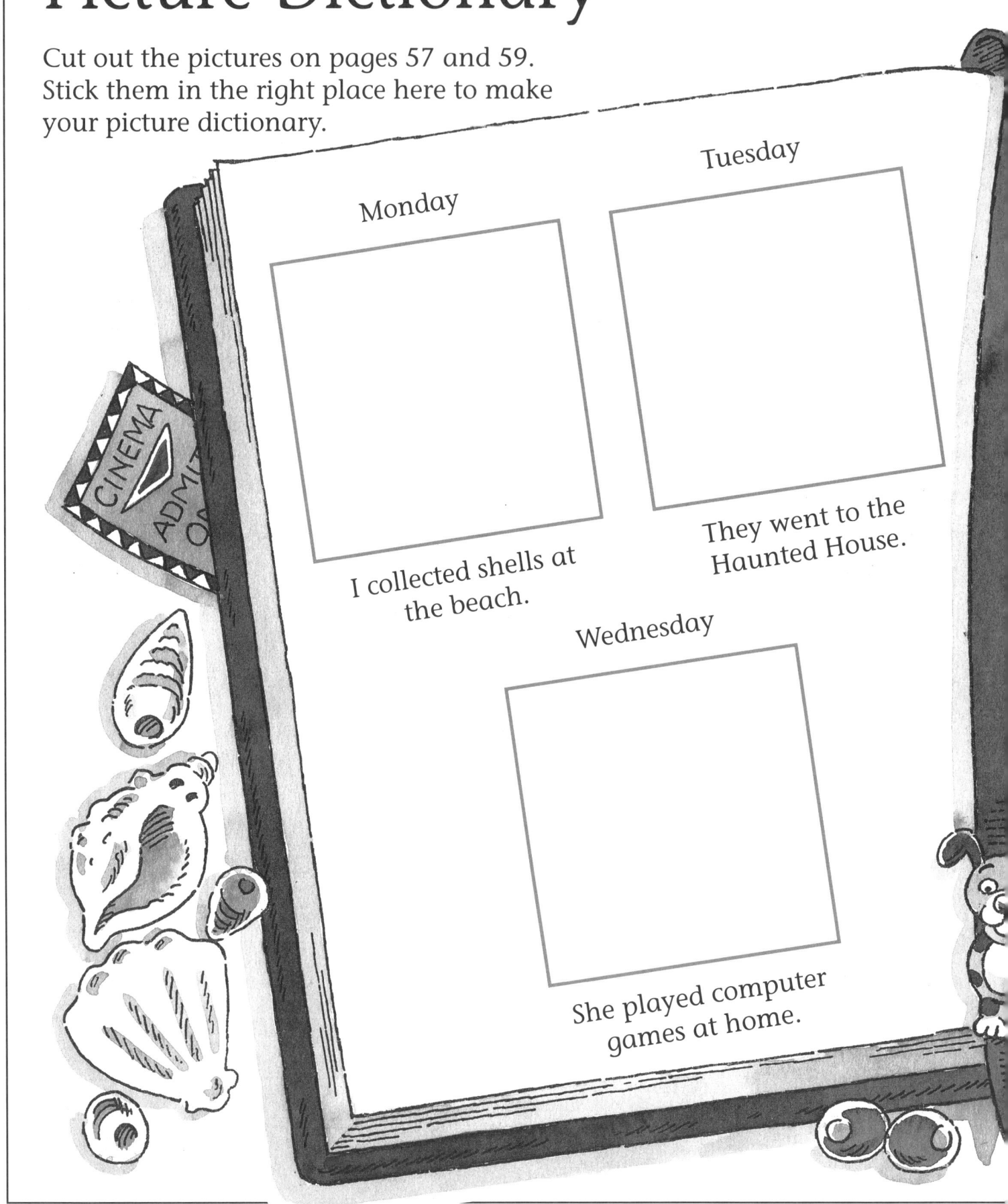

Monday

Tuesday

I collected shells at
the beach.

They went to the
Haunted House.

Wednesday

She played computer
games at home.

Thursday

Friday

I watched a film at
the cinema.

She sailed a boat at
the lake.

Saturday

Sunday

She painted a picture.

He cooked a pizza.

GREE

FUN FAIR
1 RIDE

Cut out the sentences on page 61 and stick them in
the right place here to make your picture dictionary.

Cut out these pictures and stick them in the right
place on pages 54 and 55.

Cut out these pictures and stick them in the right place on pages 54 and 55.

Cut out these sentences and stick them in the right place on page 56.

The elephant is taller than the ostrich.

The snake is longer than the tiger.

The rabbit is bigger than the frog.

The zebra is smaller than the camel.

The horse is faster than the snail.

The tortoise is slower than the lion.

My year

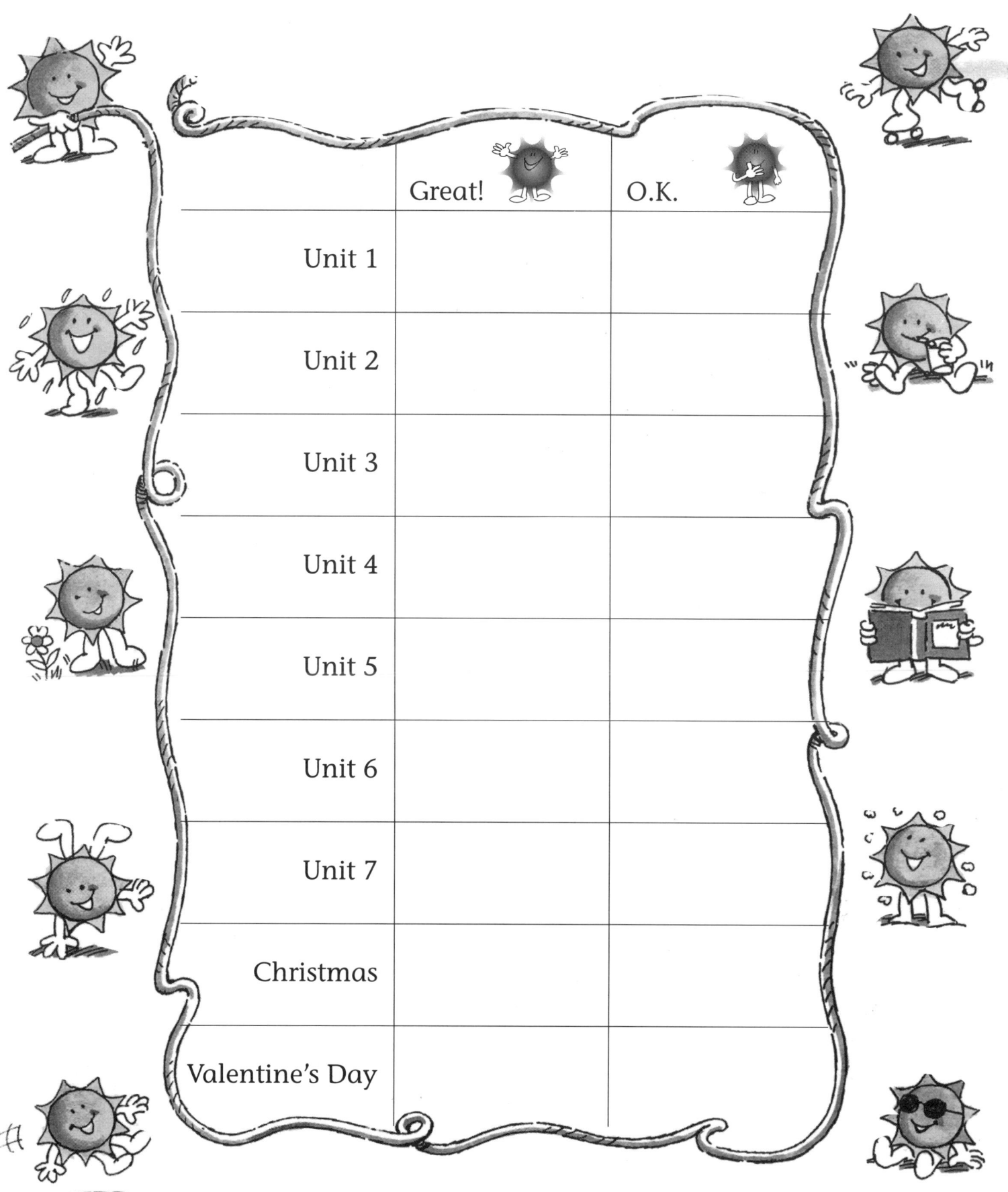

	Great!	O.K.
Unit 1		
Unit 2		
Unit 3		
Unit 4		
Unit 5		
Unit 6		
Unit 7		
Christmas		
Valentine's Day		

Macmillan Heinemann English Language Teaching, Oxford

A division of Macmillan Publishers Limited

Companies and representatives throughout the world

ISBN 0 435 29313 3

Based on the *Say It In English* language pack
© Dorling Kindersley Limited & World Book Inc.
Original material used by permission of Dorling Kindersley Limited.

Text, design and illustration © Macmillan Publishers Limited 1999
Heinemann is a registered trademark of Reed Educational & Professional Publishing Limited

First published 1999

Designed by The Junction.
Illustrated by Teri Gower and David Till

Cover illustrated by Teri Gower and designed by Sue Vaudin

Printed and bound in Great Britain by Redwood Books, Trowbridge, Wiltshire

99 00 01 02 03 10 9 8 7 6 5 4 3 2 1